Our perfect God

A summary of the attributes of God

© Day One Publications 2005
First printed 2005

ISBN 1 903087 77-5

British Library Cataloguing in Publication Data available

Published by Day One Publications
Ryelands Road, Leominster, HR6 8NZ
☎ 01568 613 740 FAX 01568 611 473
email—sales@dayone.co.uk
web site—www.dayone.co.uk
North American—e-mail—sales@dayonebookstore.com
North American—web site—www.dayonebookstore.com

Designed by Steve Devane and printed by Gutenberg Press, Malta

Contents

Contents

Commendation

Many years ago, I recall raising a question at the Westminster Fellowship, under the Chairmanship of Dr Martyn Lloyd-Jones. It concerned the relationship between the knowledge *about* God and an experiential knowledge *of* God. Of course, the purpose of the *about* is to lead us to the *of.* This *about,* Tim Shenton's sure-footed guide, in brief and clear compass, does admirably, and points the way towards the *of.* I'm grateful for this well-written and accessible study on the being and ways of God.

DR TIM BRADY

PRINCIPAL, MOORLANDS COLLEGE

Many Christians live their lives without ever seriously considering the doctrine of God. They believe that such a study is far too 'deep' for the ordinary Christian, and therefore only useful for theologians and committed Bible students. *Our perfect God* endeavours to break down that preconceived idea and to revive an interest in the being of God among ordinary Christians. While it is hoped that both ministers and students will derive much benefit from it, its principal aim is to speak to the ordinary Christian, who would normally shy away from theological subjects.

Although it is a theological work and therefore necessarily theological, I have tried to make the more complex issues as simple and as readable as possible. I have omitted lengthy arguments about controversial matters, simply stating the doctrine as I understand it. To help the reader I have included a glossary of theological terms at the back.

Throughout I follow the format adopted by the majority of systematic theology books, where, for the sake of simplicity and ease of reference, each attribute is dealt with separately and as a distinct unit. This style inevitably leads to some repetition and overlap, which I have deliberately retained so that each attribute remains complete in itself. It must be remembered, however, that the attributes are essentially one and indivisible, consistent with one another and identical with the being of God.

During the course of this study I have endeavoured to define the indefinable, to explain the infinite, to understand the incomprehensible and to describe the invisible God, who lives in 'unapproachable light, whom no one has seen or can see' (1 Timothy 6:16). This has, not surprisingly, led to a number of perplexities in my own mind, which I hope have not translated themselves onto the written page. I have been only too aware that it is an impossible task to describe God adequately and fully or to comprehend him as he really is. My prayer is, though, that through this work the reader will attain to a deeper knowledge and more personal understanding of our sovereign and almighty Lord and Saviour. To him be glory both now and for ever. Amen.

TIM SHENTON

The Westminster Confession of Faith

(Of God and of the Holy Trinity)

'There is one only living and true God, who is infinite in being and perfection. He is pure spirit, invisible, without body, parts or passions; immutable, immense, incomprehensible, eternal, almighty, most wise, most holy, most free, most absolute. He works all things according to the counsel of his own immutable and most righteous will, for his own glory. He is most loving, gracious, merciful, longsuffering, abundant in goodness and truth, forgiving iniquity, transgression and sin. He rewards all who diligently seek him. He is most just and terrible in his judgments, hating all sin. He by no means clears the guilty.

'God has all life, glory, goodness, blessedness in and of himself. He is alone all-sufficient, not needing any creature, which he has made, nor deriving any glory from them, but only manifesting his own glory in, by, to and on them. He alone is the fountain of all being, of whom, through whom and to whom are all things. He has most sovereign dominion over them to do by them, for them, or to them whatever he pleases. In his sight all things are open and manifest. His knowledge is infinite, infallible and independent of the creature, so that nothing is to him contingent or uncertain. He is most holy in all his counsels, works and commands. To him is due from angels and men, and every other creature, whatever worship, service or obedience he is pleased to require of them.'

Chapter 2 sections 1 & 2

'Now this is eternal life:
that they may know you, the only true God,
and Jesus Christ, whom you have sent' (John 17:3).

It needs to be stated from the outset that God is not just 'another' deity, existing to satisfy our religious curiosity and whims, and always ready to gratify our selfish desires. On the contrary, he is the only true and living God, who is able to do with us as he pleases. He is the creator and king of the universe, and the sole source and sustainer of all life—natural (Job 12:10; Daniel 5:23; Acts 17:28), spiritual and eternal. Without him nothing was made that has been made (John 1:3), and without a saving knowledge of him, his creatures are void of hope, and fit only to be banished from his presence for ever (2 Thessalonians 1:9).

There is no more pressing need for mankind today than to acquire a deep and personal knowledge of God. It far outweighs all the other trifles that men pursue. Nor is there a weightier question facing the world than God himself. Who is he? Is he knowable? Can he be trusted?

There is no subject more fit for our meditations than the highest and noblest Being and those transcendently glorious excellencies with which he is clothed. What incomparable sweetness will holy souls find in viewing and considering them! What immeasurable delight will we experience in seeing the most holy, the most wise, the most powerful God of all creation from whom our happiness consists! Such thoughts are the richest and loveliest the mind can entertain. They are more precious than a sea of diamonds, more to be prized than a mountain of gold; they keep the soul in perfect peace (Isaiah 26:3).

A right understanding of God is indispensable for truth and practical Christian living. There is scarcely an error in doctrine or a failure in applying Christian ethics that cannot be traced finally to imperfect and ignoble thoughts about God. These base ideas lead to an idolatrous worship of a distant and unfamiliar deity, whose altar is inscribed with the words: 'To an unknown god' (Acts 17:23). The divine attributes are not only infinitely excellent in themselves, but a grand foundation for all true divine worship, and should be the great motives to provoke men to exercise faith, love, fear and humility, and all that holy obedience they are called to by the gospel.

John Calvin opens his *Institutes of the Christian Religion* with the words: 'Nearly all the wisdom we possess, that is to say, true and sound wisdom, consists of two parts: the knowledge of God and ourselves.' As we study the divine attributes, may the God of all grace impart to us 'the Spirit of wisdom and revelation', so that we may know him better (Ephesians 1:17).

Let not the wise man boast of his wisdom
or the strong man boast of his strength
or the rich man boast of his riches,
but let him who boasts boast about this:
that he understands and knows me,
that I am the LORD, who exercises kindness,
justice and righteousness on earth,
for in these I delight
(Jeremiah 9:23–24).

The meaning of the word 'attributes'

God has so revealed himself that it is possible to ascribe certain qualities or characteristics to him. These qualities constitute his being and character, and distinguish him from all his creatures and creation. They are commonly called 'attributes'.

The word 'attributes', however, is misleading as it implies that something is added to the divine Being. The term 'properties' is favoured by some as it describes the properties of God's all-perfect nature. It is certainly more appropriate as it points to something that is proper to God and to God alone, although it still suggests a distinction between God's nature and that which is proper to it.

The word 'perfections' is probably the most suitable. It is a more biblical term and avoids the implication that something is added to the being of God. Reformed theologians define the attributes of God as those perfections which are predicated of the divine Being in Scripture, or are visibly exercised by him in his works of creation, providence and redemption. Others, whose definition is not as strict in a theological sense, say that an attribute is whatever God has revealed as being true of himself, or whatever can be correctly ascribed to God.

In this study the words 'attributes' and 'perfections' are used interchangeably.

The divine attributes

Before proceeding any further there are a number of important points that need to be made:

a. The perfections of God are, in both fact and idea, essential to and inseparable from, the nature of the divine Being, which in itself is infinite, eternal and unchangeable. God cannot be thought of apart from these perfections, for without them he would cease to be God, and yet he is more than the sum total of them all.

b. The perfections of God can only be known in the way and as far as he has condescended to reveal them. With every conception there is the element of incomprehensibility, which is inseparable from infinitude, so that even after the list of perfections that the Scripture gives is exhausted, God is still not fully defined.

c. From eternity God possessed these attributes in all their fullness, for they are co-existent and eternally unchangeable qualities of the divine Being. At no time did he acquire them and at no point did they change or evolve.

d. Although each attribute will be dealt with separately, they must never be thought of as 'parts' of God's being or disassociated from his other perfections, for God is one and indivisible.

The methods of determining the attributes of God

There are a number of ways to determine the perfections of God. One of the most popular ways is to arrange them according to the manner in which a knowledge of them is arrived. In other words, our idea of God is formed from what we know to be true about his creatures and creation. This method is summarized under three headings:

a. By the way of causation; that is, every effect in the world has a cause and the first cause is God. So from the contemplation of creation the idea of an almighty creator is formed, and from the observation of the moral government of the world comes the concept of a powerful and wise ruler. 'The heavens declare the glory of God; the skies proclaim the work of his hands' (Psalm 19:1; cf Romans 1:20).

b. By the way of negation; that is, we deny to God the limitations and imperfections that belong to his creatures, and in their place attribute to him the opposite perfection. For example, man is finite, therefore God is infinite; man is mutable, therefore God is immutable. In this way we describe God as independent, incorporeal, immortal, incomprehensible and so on.

c. By the way of eminence; that is, by exalting without limit perfections that belong to an infinite Being, or by taking man's attributes (the effect) and ascribing them in the most eminent manner to God (the cause).

* * * * * * * * * *

Although these methods appeal to some, they are not satisfactory when it comes to determining the character of God. Their principal weakness is that they start with man and his experiences, basing any knowledge of God on human conclusions, rather than relying on the self-revelation of God in his word. They exalt the idea of human discovery of God, and exaggerate man's ability to find out God and to determine his nature. Thus they drag the divine Being down to his creatures' level and create a God made in the image of man.

The only proper way of obtaining a perfectly reliable knowledge of the divine attributes is by studying the word of God. Scripture alone clearly shows us the true God.

The classification of the divine attributes
A great deal of time and energy has been spent trying to classify the divine perfections, principally to bring order and clarity to a complex subject. In an effort to maintain both God's

transcendence and his immanence, and at the same time to make a distinction between them, theologians have suggested various classifications, which usually have two groups of attributes. (On the whole these groups amount to the same thing; they are just different divisions of the same classification.) Each group is designated by a different name. None of the classifications are perfectly accurate or complete, and no single method has the universal support of Christians.

a. Absolute and relative. An absolute attribute is a property of the divine essence considered in itself, such as self-existence, immutability and eternity. It belongs to God and implies no relation to other beings or to the world. A relative attribute is a property of the divine essence considered in relation to the creation, such as omnipresence and omniscience.

b. Natural and moral. Some suggest a classification in the nature of the attributes themselves and include the idea of moral excellence. Hence the distinction natural and moral. Natural (sometimes called nonmoral) attributes, such as self-existence and eternity, are those that pertain to God as an infinite, rational Spirit; that is, they belong to his essential nature. Moral attributes, such as justice, mercy and truth, are those that belong to God as an infinite, moral being.

c. Negative and positive. Negative attributes are those that deny to God all defect and limitation of any kind. They are simplicity, infinity, eternity and immutability. Positive attributes affirm some positive perfection of God. To this group belong power, knowledge, holiness, justice, goodness and truth.

d. Essence, intellect and will. This division is taken from the constitution of man's nature. The attributes of God are arranged under three heads: those that pertain to his essence, and those that refer to his intellect and will. God, who is Spirit, is infinite, eternal and immutable in his Being, and in all that belongs to his intelligence (knowledge and wisdom) and will (power, holiness, justice, goodness and truth).

e. Incommunicable and communicable. This is the most common and historically important distinction, and the one that is adopted in this study. God's incommunicable attributes, such as self-existence, eternity and immensity, are those that have no analogy in man. His communicable attributes, such as power, knowledge, goodness and mercy, are those that find an expression in man or are reflected in other moral agents.

This distinction, however, must not be pressed too far, for all God's perfections are incommunicable because they are all infinite. At the same time, they are all communicable inasmuch as they all find some analogy in man since man was created in the image of God. Conversely, we could say that none of God's attributes are incommunicable because they are all found, albeit very faintly, in man; and none of them are communicable because none of them are found in man as they are found in God.

Although this distinction is important, it should not infer that the two groups are separate from each other; for God possesses all his attributes in an absolute way and to an infinite degree. *The Shorter Catechism of the Westminster Assembly* (1647), in answer to the question: 'What is God?', says, 'God is a spirit, infinite, eternal and unchangeable in his being, wisdom, power, holiness, justice, goodness and truth.'

The incommunicable attributes of God

The incommunicable attributes have their fullest expression in the name Elohim or God. They emphasize the absolute being of God, who is both infinite and self-sufficient, and affirm his exaltedness and incomparableness, being neither found in nor shared by his creatures. An insistence on them protects against pantheism and polytheism.

1. The self-existence of God

God is uncaused and uncreated, existing by the necessity of his own being, never needing to be created because he always was, and without any capacity or possibility ever not to be. He is the eternal One, who possesses the ground of existence in himself. He did not receive his being from another, nor did he bring himself into existence, for nothing can make itself. 'Before the mountains were born or you brought forth the earth and the world, from everlasting to everlasting you are God' (Psalm 90:2; cf Isaiah 40:28). 'In the beginning God' (Genesis 1:1).

He is the ground and first cause of all things, and it is only through him that all things exist. 'For from him and through him and to him are all things' (Romans 11:36). All things were created by him (Revelation 4:11) and are therefore dependent on him for their existence. 'He himself gives all men life and breath and everything else' (Acts 17:25). 'In him we live and move and have our being' (Acts 17:28; cf Job 12:10; Daniel 5:23). He is before all things and in him, the source and sustainer of all life, all things hold together (Colossians 1:16–17).

God exists in a different way from his creatures. We exist in a dependent, derived, finite, fragile way, but our Maker exists in an eternal, self-sustaining, necessary way—necessary, that is, in the sense that God does not have it in him to go out of existence, just as we do not have it in us to live for ever. We necessarily age and die, because it is our present nature to do that; God necessarily continues for ever unchanged, because it is his eternal nature to do that.

Some theologians use the term 'aseity', meaning that God possesses inexhaustible life in himself, which he draws from himself (John 5:26). Others prefer the term 'independence', which incorporates the idea that God has no origin with the fact that he is absolutely independent of anyone or anything outside of himself for existence. 'He is not served by human hands, as if he needed anything' (Acts 17:25). God has no cause, depends on no other and was what he is from eternity.

a. God is independent in his thought. He did not receive his knowledge from anything or anyone outside of himself. The prophet Isaiah makes this point in a very striking manner when he asks: 'Who has understood the mind [or Spirit, NIV margin] of the LORD or instructed him as his counsellor? Whom did the LORD consult to enlighten him, and who taught him the right way? Who was it that taught him knowledge or showed him the path of understanding?' (40:13–14; cf Romans 11:34; 1 Corinthians 2:16).

God is boundless and unsearchable in his knowledge (Romans 11:33), beyond any form of regulation or measurement. He is the mastermind who requires no teacher to advise or instruct him, no book to inform him about things unknown. He is perfectly independent and infinitely exalted above the supervision and direction of his creatures. He is omniscient, knowing all things even before he created them. All things depend on God's knowledge, while his knowledge depends on nothing, but is as independent as his own essence.

b. God is independent in his power. 'Our God is in heaven; he does whatever pleases him' (Psalm 115:3). He is absolutely free to act as and when he chooses, without consulting any of his creatures or requiring their approval. There are no restrictions that can be put on his power other than the ones he imposes. There are no guidelines for him to follow for its exercise, outside his own will. There is no other authority in heaven or on earth to whom he is responsible. The universe is under God's control and, being superior to every obstruction, he does freely everything that seems good to him.

c. God is independent in his counsel and will. When God acts he needs no counsellors to advise him or armies to support him. He fulfils his purposes without any necessary assistance from his creatures. Nothing he wills is ever frustrated (Job 42:2), and his counsels are immovable and infallible. 'The plans of the LORD stand firm for ever, the purposes of his heart through all generations' (Psalm 33:11). The First Cause of all things holds all second causes in his hand, and can subvert any plot in a moment even by means and instruments esteemed the most contemptible. 'The LORD foils the plans of the nations, he thwarts the purposes of the peoples' (Psalm 33:10).

There are no events in this world that are not directed by his hand 'in accordance with his pleasure and will' (Ephesians 1:5; cf 1:11). There are no 'accidents' that reside outside his control (Matthew 10:29). He is self-governing and without obligation to his creatures. 'He does as he pleases with the powers of heaven and the peoples of the earth. No one can hold back his hand or say to him: "What have you done?"' (Daniel 4:35). His will is irresistible (Romans 9:19) and all his creatures are subject to and governed by it. If anything could frustrate or change God's will, it would be superior to God, and therefore God would not be God.

2. The immutability of God

'In the beginning you laid the foundations of the earth, and the heavens are the work of your hands. They will perish, but you remain; they will all wear out like a garment. Like clothing you will change them and they will be discarded. But you remain the same, and your years will never end' (Psalm 102:25–27; cf Hebrews 1:10–12). 'I the LORD do not change' (Malachi 3:6). The Father of the heavenly lights does not change like shifting shadows (James 1:17).

a. God is immutable in his essence. God is both immutable in himself and unchangeable by anything outside himself. His nature and being are subject to no mutations, no process of development, no self-evolution. He is eternally exalted above every cause and effect and entirely separate from any possibility of change. He cannot grow, decay, improve or deteriorate. He is perpetually the same and can never cease to be God.

Any change is always for better or worse. God cannot change for better because he is already perfect, and being perfect he cannot change for worse. He did not make himself, nor did anyone else make him, for he has always been what he is. He cannot change himself or be changed by others, for his being is unalterably fixed. He is 'the same yesterday and today and for ever' (Heb.13:8); 'the Alpha and the Omega, the First and the Last, the Beginning and the End' (Revelation 22:13; cf Isaiah

41:4; 48:12) in whom there is no variableness or shadow of turning. Being infinite in duration he cannot know succession and, being uninfluenced by time, he cannot age. He is 'from all eternity' (Psalm 93:2) the 'immortal God' (Romans 1:23).

b. God is immutable in all his perfections. The very term 'perfections' indicates their eternal immutability. What they are today is what they have always been and always will be, without increase and incapable of diminishing. God is immutable and, as his perfections coincide with his being, they can no more change than God himself. God's perfections are infinite and nothing can be added to or taken from the infinite.

God can never know more or less than he has always known for he is omniscient (John 21:17). He has known all things from the beginning and nothing in all creation is hidden from his sight (Hebrews 4:13). He can never become more or less powerful for he is eternally omnipotent. Nothing is too hard for him (Jeremiah 32:17, cf. Genesis 18:14). He is 'the only wise God' (Romans 16:27) whose 'love endures for ever' (Psalm 118:29). He is 'rich in mercy' and grace (Ephesians 2:4,7), 'majestic in holiness' (Exodus 15:11) and faithful through all generations (Psalm 119:90). His word of truth 'stands firm in the heavens' (Psalm 119:89), unalterable and unbreakable (John 10:35), never to be updated or revised. He is constant in all his perfections and therefore utterly dependable in his relations and faithful to his covenants.

c. God is immutable in his counsel. God's decree stands as an immovable mountain, founded on infallible wisdom and supported by unrestricted power. His eternal purpose is unchanging in nature (Hebrews 6:17), his promises never fail and his plans are executed without modification. His 'gifts and his call are irrevocable' (Romans 11:29). 'He stands alone, and who can oppose him? He does whatever he pleases' (Job 23:13; cf. Isaiah 55:11). 'God is not a man, that he should lie, nor a son of man, that he should change his mind. Does he speak and then not act? Does he promise and not fulfil?' (Numbers 23:19; cf 1 Samuel 15:29).

What he performs in time he planned from eternity, and what he planned in eternity he carries out in time. He is omniscient and therefore alternative plans are unnecessary and, being omnipotent, he always possesses sufficient power to see them through. 'Many are the plans in a man's heart, but it is the LORD's purpose that prevails' (Proverbs 19:21). 'Surely, as I have planned, so it will be, and as I have purposed, so it will stand,' says the LORD (Isaiah 14:24; cf 46:10–11).

* * * * * * * * * *

One of the objections raised about the immutability of God is that a number of passages in the Bible seem to ascribe change to God. He appears to change his mind (Exodus 32:14; Jonah 3:10), to repent of his actions (Genesis 6:6; 1 Samuel 15:35), and to deal with the faithful and crooked in a different manner (Psalm 18:25–27). He also created the world and became incarnate in Christ, and these things appear irreconcilable with immutability.

Immutability, however, is not incompatible with mobility. God cannot change in his being, perfections, promises or purpose, but he does act and move. He does not change his will, but he does change his work. When a change occurs, it is not a change in God, for his will and essence are the same, but a change in man and in his relations to God. Creation was the eternal, immutable purpose of God which, when realised by an act of his will, brought about no change in God. The change was in the creature, which began to be what it was not before. God always acts upon his creatures according to his immutable, holy and just nature. Hence the innocent are the objects of his kindness and the wicked the objects of his wrath.

The incarnation, when the eternal, pre-existent Son of God assumed a distinct and created human nature into personal union with himself, caused no change in God's being or perfections. There was a union of the two natures, but no change of deity into humanity or of humanity into deity; both preserved their peculiar properties. Another writer comments that a cloud over the sun makes no change in the body of the sun; so, though the divine nature be covered with the human, it makes no change in the divine nature. Nor was there a change in God's purpose, for it was his eternal good pleasure to send his Son into the world.

When God speaks of himself he often uses anthropomorphic language. For instance, he describes himself as having 'hands' (Isaiah 45:12), 'feet' (Isaiah 37:25), 'eyes' (Jeremiah 16:17) and 'nostrils' (Isaiah 65:5). These are figurative expressions, or human ways of speaking, which are used by God to help us understand the greatness of his perfections and actions. They must never be taken literally, and always be interpreted in a way that agrees with the infinite excellency and majesty of God.

So when he appears to change his mind, as in Jonah 3:10, he is simply describing the events in an easy-to-follow way. There has been no change in his will, only in man's relation to him. The word of destruction he uttered against the Ninevites was not an absolute but a conditional word to bring them to repentance. Then, when they turned from their evil ways, he had compassion on them, thus fulfilling his eternal purpose.

3. The infinity of God

It is not possible for our finite human minds to understand that which has no limits or restrictions. 'Can you fathom the mysteries of God? Can you probe the limits of the Almighty? They are higher than the heavens—what can you do? They are deeper than the depths of the grave—what can you know? Their measure is longer than the earth and wider than the sea' (Job 11:7–9). God is infinitely greater than the human mind and beyond the description of the most eloquent pen. All we can hope to achieve is to submit and be content with the truth about God as far as we comprehend it.

The infinity of God means that God, in his being and perfections, is absolutely free from all limitations, conditions and defects. He is not limited by time or space, or confined to or by the universe. The heavens, even the highest heaven, cannot contain him (1 Kings 8:27). There are two aspects of God's infinity that need to be distinguished:

a. His eternity. The infinity of God in relation to time is called his eternity. Throughout the Bible God is called 'eternal' or 'everlasting', and referred to in ways that emphasise this aspect of his infinity. 'Now to the King eternal, immortal, invisible, the only God, be honour and glory for ever and ever' (1 Timothy 1:17). 'You are from all eternity' (Psalm 93:2). 'The LORD is the everlasting God' (Isaiah 40:28), who will no more have an end than he had a beginning. He is the first and the last (Isaiah 44:6), the Alpha and the Omega (Revelation 21:6), 'who lives for ever' (Isaiah 57:15) and whose kingdom and throne endure through all generations (Psalm 145:13; Hebrews 1:8).

God is eternal. He always was, always is, and always will be what he is. He is permanent, remaining entire and constant in his being and perfections through all times. He is unchanged in an infinite duration and without succession in all his thoughts, feelings, purposes and acts.

God is exalted above time and all its limitations. He exists outside the bounds of time and, although he is its author, he is not conditioned, confined or measured by it (Psalm 90:2,4; 2 Peter 3:8). For him there is no past or future, no moment before or after him, only an eternal present. Time is an eternal 'now' and he is the eternal 'I AM' (Exodus 3:14; cf Revelation 1:4,8). All things are equally and always present to his view. In other words, God possesses the whole of his endless existence in one indivisible present.

b. His immensity. The infinity of God in relation to space is called his immensity (or his omnipresence). God, in the totality of his being, is simultaneously present every moment of time at every point of space. Or to put it another way, God is present by his essence in all places in heaven and on earth at once. 'Heaven is my throne, and the earth is my footstool' (Isaiah 66:1).

David establishes the immensity of God when he says: 'Where can I go from your Spirit? Where can I flee from your presence? If I go up to the heavens, you are there; if I make my bed in the depths, you are there. If I rise on the wings of the dawn, if I settle on the far side of the sea, even there your hand will guide me, your right hand will hold me fast' (Psalm 139:7–10).

God transcends all spatial limitations. He is not confined to any one point of space, or excluded or absent from any part of it. There is no part of space where his whole substance does not exist all the time. He is not more present in one part than in another, nor is he bounded, preserved or sustained in any way by it. He fills all space absolutely and eternally, and yet he is more vast than it all. There is no place that can compass or contain him (1 Kings 8:27) and he dwells in all his creatures without distinction. In a word, he 'fills everything in every way' (Ephesians 1:23; cf Jeremiah 23:23–24).

Although God is equally omnipresent at all times to all his creatures, he manifests his presence and exercises his power at different times and in a variety of degrees and modes. And although he is immanent in all his creatures, he is not present in them in the same sense. For instance, he does not dwell on earth as he does in heaven, in animals as he does in man, in the wicked as he does in the righteous, nor in the church as he does in Christ. He has a presence of glory in heaven, where he comforts the saints, and a presence of wrath in hell, where he torments the damned.

The immensity of God does not mean that he is diffused through space, with one part of his being in one place and another part in some other place, for Spirit is not composed of parts. God is not capable of extension because he is ever one and indivisible, always simple and inseparable. He cannot multiply his essence or make himself greater than he was before because he is infinite; that is, he is already in entirety in all places. Nor does the doctrine of immensity teach that God is everything and everything is God; or that he is present in creation only in knowledge and power and not by his essence, and therefore acts upon the world from a distance. These are errors that the Christian must guard against.

God, who is infinite in being, does not absorb created beings into his essence, although he creates, preserves and governs all things. He does not mingle with his creatures or blend together with them, but remains for ever distinct. God does not intermix with created matter, nor is he contaminated by its impurities. He is in all and over all, yet essentially separate from and independent of all.

Although the terms 'immensity' and 'omnipresence' are generally regarded as synonymous, there is an important difference between them. 'Immensity' is the infinity of God in relation to space viewed abstractly in itself, or as belonging to deity from eternity. It emphasises the transcendence of God, who is over and beyond creation, and who is not subject to spatial limitations. 'Omnipresence' is the infinity of God in relation to his creatures. God is equally present with all his creatures at all times and in all places. This term stresses the immanence of God, who is acting within and through creation, and filling every part of space with his entire being.

4. The unity of God

a. God is unique. There is only one true and living God. He is numerically one and there are no other gods like him. This is expressly stated throughout the Bible. 'Acknowledge and take to heart this day that the LORD is God in heaven above and on earth below. There is no other' (Deuteronomy 4:39; cf 1 Kings 8:60). 'Hear, O Israel: The LORD our God, the LORD is one' (Deuteronomy 6:4; cf Mark 12:29). 'I am the first and I am the last; apart from me there is no God' (Isaiah 44:6; cf 45:21). 'You are right in saying that God is one and there is no other but him' (Mark 12:32; cf 1 Corinthians 8:4,6). There is 'one God and Father of all, who is over all and through all and in all' (Ephesians 4:6; cf 1 Timothy 2:5).

The uniqueness of God follows from the fact that there can only be one absolute and infinite being. You cannot, for instance, have two infinite beings who 'fill heaven and earth' (Jeremiah 23:24). If one infinite being fills all space at once, then there is no room for another. Or if one infinite being possesses all power, there is no power left for a second infinite being. If there were two infinite beings, each would necessarily include the other, and thus they would be the same, one and identical. This doctrine excludes polytheistic notions of God.

b. God is simple. By describing God as 'simple' we mean that the three persons in the Godhead are numerically one essence and constitute one indivisible God (John 10:30); that is, they are not three parts of which the divine essence is composed, but one self-existent and immutable God.

Although the three persons are distinguishable from each other, they cannot be divided in any sense for God is one. The Father, Son and Spirit are one God, three in one and one in three. In God's essence reside three persons in whom one God is known. Nor are there any degrees in the Godhead, for each person possesses the entire essence of God and dwells wholly in the other persons. Thus the three persons are coequal, coeternal and coexistent.

Not only are the three persons in the Godhead one, without division or inferiority, but God and his attributes are one as well. His essence and perfections are identical. The Bible often identifies the being of God with his perfections, thus stressing this unity: God is light (1 John 1:5), God is love (1 John 4:16), God is life (1 John 5:20) and so on.

The communicable attributes of God

While the incommunicable attributes stress the absolute being of God, the communicable attributes emphasise his perfect personal nature. Perfect personality is found only in God, and what we see in man is only a finite copy of the original. Moreover, there is a tri-personality in God, of which no analogy is found in human beings. There are three main arguments for the personality of God:

a. The argument from design. The world everywhere exhibits design. Its order and harmony, which are the effects of reason and counsel, as well as the complex system of the universe, all point to an eternal and absolute cause of everything, who possesses infinite intelligence, benevolence, will and power, which are the marks of personality. 'God made the earth by his power; he founded the world by his wisdom and stretched out the heavens by his understanding' (Jeremiah 10:12).

b. The argument from man's nature. The cause of man's personality must be personal, otherwise the effect is superior to the cause. Our moral nature, which is innate in all of us, imposes on us a sense of right and wrong, and an obligation to obey the law and therefore a lawgiver, who knows us and demands an account from us. It forces us to believe in a personal God on whom we are dependent and to whom we are responsible. Our religious nature prompts us to seek out a higher being to whom we can be faithful, loving and obedient. These desires necessitate a personal God in whose image we are made. The whole frame of our bodies and souls bears the impress of the infinite power and wisdom of the Creator; a body framed with an admirable architecture and a soul endowed with understanding, will, judgment, memory and imagination.

c. The argument from Scripture. Although the word 'person' is not applied to God in the Bible, there are numerous evidences of his divine personality therein: his presence with his people in the Old and New Testaments; the anthropomorphic expressions that are applied to him; his perfections, titles and names, especially the name LORD; the personal pronouns that refer to him; man's ability to have an intimate relationship with him; and the life, work and personality of his Son, Jesus Christ. The Bible also describes how God enters our experiences, relieves our suffering, acts on our behalf, grieves over sin, knows all things and wills self-consciously, all of which are in accordance with our concept of personality.

1. The spirituality of God

The nearest to a definition of God that the Bible comes is John 4:24: 'God is spirit, and his worshippers must worship in spirit and in truth.' God is not 'a' spirit but pure Spirit. He has an undefiled, unmixed, uncreated spiritual essence that is without material substance and free from all limitations and imperfections. As Spirit he cannot be extended or divided into parts, and is in no way tangible. None of the attributes of matter or flesh can be ascribed to him for he is without composition. He is distinct from the world, wholly separate from anything corporeal and is indiscernible by the bodily senses (1 Corinthians 2:11–14).

Whatever is essential to the idea of Spirit, as we understand it, is to be applied to God in an infinite degree; that is, the properties of our own spirits must be ascribed to God without limit. On this basis, God is a rational, intelligent, free and moral person who is self-conscious and self-determining. He is all-powerful, supremely wise and loving, and the possessor of all the qualities that belong to perfect, infinite Spirit. He is not an impersonal force or power, but the most spiritual Spirit.

God is without flesh or bones or bodily parts. In the Bible the bodily members that are ascribed to God are anthropomorphic expressions, which are figuratively or metaphorically applied to him in order to aid our understanding of him. God, as it were, humbles his own nature to suit and assist the capacity of the creature. God's 'right hand', for instance, refers to the operations of his strong power and 'the eyes of the LORD' symbolize his omniscience. Such representations usually, but not exclusively, communicate his visible actions rather than his invisible nature.

Although these analogies with human beings shed light on the spiritual, they must never be taken literally. The design and not the letter of the metaphors must govern our conceptions of God, for he is uncreated and invisible Spirit, and infinitely greater than and distinct from his creatures. '"To whom will you compare me? Or who is my equal?" says the Holy One' (Isaiah 40:25). The human body is limited by time and space: God is both immense and eternal. The body is weak and often damaged: God is omnipotent and impassible. The body is dependent on God for life: God is self-existent. Article 1 of the Church of England states: 'There is but one living and true God, everlasting, without body, parts or passions; of infinite power, wisdom and goodness.'

The only 'image of God', in whom some figurative expressions were literally fulfilled (cf Psalm 78:2 with Matthew

13:34–35), is Jesus Christ (2 Corinthians 4:4; Colossians 1:15), who shares in our humanity (Hebrews 2:14). 'The Son is the radiance of God's glory and the exact representation of his being... he was made a little lower than the angels' (Hebrews 1:3; 2:9). 'In the beginning was the Word, and the Word was with God, and the Word was God... the Word became flesh and lived for a while among us' (John 1:1,14). He who is 'in very nature God' (Philippians 2:6), has made known to us the 'eternal, immortal, invisible' Spirit (1 Timothy 1:17; cf 6:16; John 1:18).

2. The knowledge of God

God's knowledge is his intellectual apprehension of truth and can be described as one eternal, all-comprehensive, indivisible act of intuition. It is that perfection in God whereby he, in an entirely unique manner, knows himself and all things possible and actual in one eternal and most simple act. 'Lord, you know all things' (John 21:17). 'The LORD is a God who knows, and by him deeds are weighed' (1 Samuel 2:3). 'Can anyone teach knowledge to God, since he judges even the highest' (Job 21:22).

a. The knowledge of God is eternal and immutable. God has always known and will always know all things, for he is omniscient. He knew all things before they existed as finite realities in time and space, and he will know all things after they have crumbled into dust. If he did not know all things before they came to pass, he would gain a knowledge of them when they came to pass. And if he did not know all things after they ceased to be, he would lose a knowledge of them when they ceased to be. Thus he would either grow or diminish in knowledge and suffer a change—a very unworthy concept of the most blessed, perfect and infinite God! Everything has been 'known for ages' (Acts 15:18; cf Isaiah 45:21; 46:10) and nothing is forgotten by him.

God's knowledge coincides with his eternal and immutable essence, and is therefore permanent and unchangeable. Time does not erode it, nor, because it is perfect, can it increase or decrease.

b. The knowledge of God is independent. God does not obtain his knowledge from anything outside of himself. He does not depend in any way on secondary causes or effects, or acquire any new knowledge from any of his creatures or their actions at any time. He needs no witnesses or informants, no wise men or counsellors (Isaiah 40:13–14). He depends solely and absolutely on his own infinite knowledge, which he possesses within his own mind and will.

c. The knowledge of God is simultaneous and immediate. It is one single, indivisible act of knowing and comprehending all things in themselves, their relations and successions, as ever present actualities. All knowledge is immediately, directly and fully before his mind. He knows all past events and all future things as if they were now present. He sees all things at once in their totality, and not as successive events, although he views them as successive in time. Such knowledge does not result from observation or from a process of deduction, but is innate within the divine being.

d. The knowledge of God is perfect and infallible. 'Do you know how the clouds hang poised, those wonders of him who is perfect in knowledge?' (Job 37:16). God is perfectly acquainted with every detail in the life of every creature in heaven and on earth. There is nothing that escapes his notice, nothing that is obscure to him. 'He knows what lies in darkness, and light dwells with him' (Daniel 2:22). The open and hidden; the past, present and future; the unimportant and the significant; his creatures from the highest to the lowest—all are equally and completely known by him. 'Even the very hairs of your head are all numbered' (Matthew 10:30).

There is no shadow or error in his knowledge, no room for improvement, nothing that he overlooks. He never learns, never discovers, never makes a mistake. He knows all things as they really are, the actual as actual, the possible as possible, the free as free and so on. He is never surprised and his understanding is as unfailing as his word. He is no more capable of error in his understanding than of imperfection in his essence; his counsels are as unerring as his essence is perfect and his knowledge as infallible as his essence is free from defect.

e. *The knowledge of God is infinite and all-comprehensive.* God literally 'knows everything' (1 John 3:20), even that which is unknowable to everyone else. 'Great is [the] LORD and mighty in power; his understanding has no limit' (Psalm 147:5 ; cf Isaiah 40:28). God, the infinite, knows himself infinitely (1 Corinthians 2:10–11; cf Matthew 11:27), which necessarily means that he possesses a limitless knowledge and perfect understanding of his own eternal being. By knowing himself, the cause of all things, he inevitably knows all things.

There are no bounds to his knowledge. He knows all things about all things—their natures, causes, virtues, operations and their relation to other things. He knows whatever is knowable. Every thought, action, word, feeling, desire, mystery and secret is before him, as well as everything else that has ever or will ever exist anywhere in the universe and beyond. 'O LORD, you have searched me and you know me. You know when I sit and when I rise; you perceive my thoughts from afar. You discern my going out and my lying down; you are familiar with all my ways. Before a word is on my tongue you know it completely, O LORD.' 'Such knowledge is too wonderful for me, too lofty for me to attain' (Psalm 139:1–4,6).

'Nothing in all creation is hidden from God's sight. Everything is uncovered and laid bare' before his eyes (Hebrews 4:13; cf Job 28:24)—the sins of his creatures (Jeremiah 16:17; cf 29:23), 'the deep things of darkness' (Job 12:22; cf Psalm 139:12), the 'longings' and 'sighings' of men (Psalm 38:9). Man looks at the outward appearance, but God searches the heart (1 Samuel 16:7; cf Luke 16:15) and examines the mind (Jeremiah 17:10). He knows all the thoughts of men (Psalm 94:11; Ezekiel 11:5) and 'understands every motive behind the thoughts' (1 Chronicles 28:9). He observes our ways (Job 24:23) and watches over our 'every step' (Job 31:4; cf Psalm 33:15). He knows how we are formed, remembering that we are dust (Psalm 103:14; cf 139:15–16). He sees our sorrows (Exodus 3:7), hears our complaints (Numbers 14:27), knows where we stay and when we come and go (2 Kings 19:27), and calls us by our names (Isaiah 45:4).

The all-comprehensive knowledge of God means that he knows all things actual and all things possible. He knows whatever might occur under certain circumstances, because he knows what his own power can effect. He knows what he could create as well as what he has created. Just as his power is infinite and can create innumerable worlds and creatures, so his knowledge is infinite in knowing all the innumerable things possible to his power. He also knows what actually takes place in space and time, because he knows what his own will has determined, and because he 'works out everything in conformity with the purpose of his will' (Ephesians 1:11).

The omniscience of God follows from his omnipresence. If

God fills heaven and earth and is in every part of space all the time, then all things necessarily take place in his presence. Moreover, if he was not omniscient, he could not govern the world with righteousness or judge the peoples with equity, for justice is based on knowledge.

* * * * * * * * * *

Before proceeding to look at the wisdom of God, a word must be said about the foreknowledge of God. Some, in an attempt to reconcile God's foreknowledge and man's freedom, deny that God has any foreknowledge of free actions, arguing that he voluntarily abstains from foreknowing them; others simply deny man's moral freedom. Both extremes are wrong. If man's freedom is understood, not as something arbitrary and uncertain, but as reasonable self-determination, then its apparent inconsistency with God's foreknowledge is more easily resolved.

The foreknowledge of God is clearly taught in many Bible passages. 'See, the former things have taken place, and new things I declare; before they spring into being I announce them to you' (Isaiah 42:9). 'I told you these things long ago; before they happened I announced them to you' (Isaiah 48:5). 'Before I formed you in the womb I knew you' (Jeremiah 1:5). 'There is a God in heaven who reveals mysteries. He has shown King Nebuchadnezzar what will happen in days to come' (Daniel 2:28; cf 1 Samuel 23:10–12; Isaiah 46:10; Matthew 11:22,24; 24:36; Acts 15:17–18). In addition, God has often predicted future contingent events that have come to pass (Matthew 20:18–19; 26:31–34).

The distinction between knowledge and foreknowledge is

only in us. God knows all things in himself from eternity, including the free acts of men and all conditional events. All his creatures and their actions as well as the past, present and future are perfectly and immediately known by him. This knowledge is absolutely independent, resting in no way on the acts of men, while nothing outside himself restricts or conditions his freedom to do as he pleases.

God has decreed all things, and has decreed them with their causes and conditions in the exact order in which they come to pass. His foreknowledge of future things and also of contingent events rests on his decree (Acts 2:23; 4:27–28; Romans 9:16; Ephesians 1:11; Philippians 2:13). As he knows his own decree and will, he inevitably knows all future things. In short, God foreordains and foreknows all things, including future contingencies and the free acts of men.

3. The wisdom of God

Although knowledge and wisdom are closely related, there is a difference: knowledge is theoretical, wisdom is practical. Wisdom presupposes knowledge, and is the practical use which the intelligence and will make of knowledge. It is the possession of experience and understanding, together with the power of applying them to ensure that the best and noblest ends are achieved. Wisdom fixes the right purpose, chooses the most fit means and directs them to the highest end. It results from an intuitive insight into things, and consists in willing and acting according to sound judgments.

God's wisdom is his ability to choose, from all possible alternatives and with perfect discernment, the highest goal, and to select and direct the best means to accomplish that goal. It is his application of knowledge to fulfil his purpose in ways that glorify himself and bring the highest good to his creatures. He chooses the right ends and means for the right reasons, and directs and arranges all things in accordance with his purposes for them. In this way he makes all things subservient to his own glory. The knowledge and wisdom of God might be explained as that essential property of God whereby, by one simple and eternal act, he knows both himself and all possible things perfectly, and according to which he makes, directs and orders all future things for his own glory.

God's wisdom, as with his other perfections, is infinite and everlasting and identical with his essence. He has through all eternity solely and wholly possessed boundless wisdom (Romans 16:27; cf Job 12:13). This means that he has never acquired any part of it or studied for it, nor has it been added in any measure to his essence. It also means that he is and was and always will be the only source and fountain of wisdom in his creatures (Daniel 2:21).

There is no defect in his wisdom and there is no act of his that could ever be done more wisely. His wisdom is pure, loving and good, and, because it unites with his power, it never fails. He sees the end from the beginning and in all things moves towards a predestined end. This inevitably removes any guesswork or risk from weakening the divine purpose. The Bible calls his wisdom 'profound' (Job 9:4). It is manifested in his works of creation, providence and redemption.

a. In creation. 'How many are your works, O LORD! In wisdom you made them all; the earth is full of your creatures' (Psalm 104:24). 'God made the earth by his power; he founded the world by his wisdom and stretched out the heavens by his understanding' (Jeremiah 10:12; cf 51:15; Proverbs 3:19).

The world with its beauty, diversity and order is a window

through which we contemplate divine wisdom. The usefulness and fitness of every part; the complexity and yet harmony of the human body; the colour and variety of flowers and trees, birds and animals—their shapes, sizes, behaviour and qualities—all wonderfully equipped and suited to their habitations; the rugged mountains, the rolling hills, the meadows and valleys that teem with natural splendour; the sea and its raging waters that never overflow their boundaries (Job 38:8–11); the seasons of the year (Psalm 74:17), day and night, seedtime and harvest (Genesis 8:22), all that grows and shines and moves (Psalm 19:1–6)—the whole of creation announces the infinite, manifold and universal wisdom of God.

b. In divine providence. 'The LORD is faithful to his promises and loving towards all he has made. The LORD upholds all those who fall and lifts up all who are bowed down. The eyes of all look to you, and you give them their food at the proper time. You open your hand and satisfy the desires of every living thing' (Psalm 145:13–16).

The LORD governs the kingdoms of the earth (Psalm 67:4) according to his will and law, and preserves both man and beast (Psalm 36:6). He directs unreasonable creatures to their appointed end, and rules over the actions and wrath of wicked men for his own praise and glory (Psalm 76:10). With an outstretched arm he 'foils the plans of the nations' (Psalm 33:10), and makes them subservient to his will. He uses sinful instruments to accomplish his purposes, brings good to his creatures out of sin, and exploits the devil and his schemes for his own ends.

He orders the paths of his people and provides them with all they need (Acts 14:17) for life and godliness (2 Peter 1:3). In everything he works for their good (Romans 8:28), ensuring that his designs for them come to pass. He rescues them from every evil attack and, through many dangers, brings them safely to his heavenly kingdom (2 Timothy 4:18).

c. In redemption. The admirable plan and execution of our redemption, whereby the justice of God is satisfied in punishing our sins and the mercy of God poured out in pardoning the sinner (Romans 3:24–25), is 'God's secret wisdom, a wisdom that has been hidden and that God destined for our glory before time began' (1 Corinthians 2:7). This wisdom satisfied both the honour and righteousness of the law. The former was satisfied by Christ's perfect obedience, the latter by his vicarious suffering on the cross; for obedience was our debt to the law as creatures and punishment was our due from the law as sinners.

From the incarnation, when the Word became flesh, to the death of the sinless Saviour, the wisdom of God shines forth. It is perfect wisdom that makes death the way to life and shame the path to glory; infinite wisdom that reconciles a holy God to sinful men, and from them creates a universal church (Ephesians 3:10)—to the praise of his glory (Ephesians 1:6); divine wisdom that fits the mediator with two natures for him to accomplish our redemption and overthrow the empire of the devil; and glorious wisdom that makes him who had no sin to be sin for us, so that in him we might become the righteousness of God (2 Corinthians 5:21). Christ Jesus, the Son of God and Saviour of the world, is the personal wisdom of God (1 Corinthians 1:24,30).

Not only that, but the divine wisdom is clearly displayed by the 'foolishness' of preaching to reach the lost and by the condition set to enjoy the fruits of redemption—repentance and faith (Mark 1:15). 'Oh, the depth of the riches of the wisdom and knowledge of God!' (Romans 11:33).

4. The truth of God

The truth of God is his essential property whereby, in his nature and works, he is utterly sincere and faithful, and completely free from any falsehood or pretence. 'He is the Rock, his works are perfect, and all his ways are just. A faithful God who does no wrong, upright and just is he' (Deuteronomy 32:4; cf Jeremiah 10:10). He is the 'God of truth' (Isaiah 65:16; cf Psalm 31:5), who abounds in love and faithfulness (Psalm 86:15). 'For great is your love, higher than the heavens; your faithfulness reaches to the skies' (Psalm 108:4; cf 57:10).

a. He is true in his being and morals. He is the only true God (John 17:3; cf 1 John 5:20), who is without deceit, hypocrisy or infidelity. He is self-consistent and, unlike the heathen gods and idols, he is what he declares himself to be. He is all that he should be and in him the concept of God is perfectly realised. There is nothing true except what is in him or what comes from him. He is the source of all truth—all moral, intellectual, religious and scientific truth—and thus the ground of the Christian's hope and faith.

Truth is the common property of his intellectual and moral attributes. He knows all things as they really are. Thus his knowledge is perfectly accurate, his wisdom is unbiased and infallible, and his goodness and justice are true to his perfect nature. In him there are no double standards or favouritisms.

b. He is true in his word. 'Your word is truth' (John 17:17). 'The word of the LORD is right and true' (Psalm 33:4). God is true in all his communications (Isaiah 45:19), whether written, oral or visionary. His word contains no flaw, deception or corruption. It is perfect truth in which God reveals himself as he really is. Its history is authentic and certain (Luke 1:3–4) and its commands are free from injustice or error. 'The law of the LORD is perfect, reviving the soul. The statutes of the LORD are trustworthy, making wise the simple. The precepts of the LORD are right, giving joy to the heart. The commands of the LORD are radiant, giving light to the eyes. … The ordinances of the LORD are sure and altogether righteous' (Psalm 19:7–9).

The Bible is true because its author is the God of truth. God cannot lie (1 Samuel 15:29; Titus 1:2; Hebrews 6:18) or pervert the truth in any way. His nature is truth itself and he cannot speak out of character. He is stable and unchanging, ever true to his truth. As a result, his word never disappoints or fails. It stands for ever (1 Peter 1:25). 'O Sovereign LORD, you are God! Your words are trustworthy' (2 Samuel 7:28).

c. He is true in his faithfulness. 'You are mighty, O LORD, and your faithfulness surrounds you' (Psalm 89:8; cf Lamentations 3:23; Exodus 34:6). 'All the ways of the LORD are loving and faithful for those who keep the demands of his covenant' (Psalm 25:10). For God to act unfaithfully would be contrary to his nature; so even if we are faithless, he remains faithful, for he cannot disown himself (2 Timothy 2:13; cf Psalm 89:33). As the Psalmist says, he 'remains faithful for ever' (Psalm 146:6; cf 119:90).

There is never any failing or falling short of his promises (1 Kings 8:56; Psalm 145:13), for no matter how many promises he has made, they are 'Yes' in Christ (2 Corinthians 1:20). He is always mindful of his covenant, keeping it to a thousand generations of those who love him and obey his commands (Deuteronomy 7:9). 'I will not violate my covenant or alter what my lips have uttered' (Psalm 89:34). He fulfils the words of his prophets and executes the threats he makes against the wicked (Zechariah 1:6). No word that goes out from his mouth returns to him empty, for it always accomplishes what he desires and achieves the purpose for which he sent it (Isaiah 55:11). His word is his bond (Hebrews 10:23), unchangeable and unshakeable.

Such faithfulness is the basis of our confidence in God and the cause of rejoicing. It is our shield and rampart (Psalm 91:4) on which rests the hope of eternal life. In times of trial and darkness it keeps us from despair and instils in us a perseverance that cries, 'Never give up!'

5. The goodness of God

The nature of God is pre-eminently characterised by goodness. In fact, pure and perfect goodness is the royal prerogative of God alone. He is good—good in himself, good in his essence, good in the highest degree, and the possessor of whatever is pleasant, excellent and desirable. Whatever is perfect goodness is God and whatever is truly goodness in any creature is a resemblance of God. In him there is nothing but good and only good proceeds from him. God exercises his goodness in various modes—love, grace, mercy, forbearance—according to the relations and conditions of his creatures. (In this work each aspect of God's goodness is dealt with separately.)

God is necessarily and altogether good in himself. He is as necessarily good as he is necessarily God, for his goodness is inseparable from his eternal being. He answers perfectly to the ideal expressed in the word 'God', being in every way all that he should be as God. He is in himself absolute moral perfection and perfect bliss. He is all-good and alone-good, and the highest good for all his creatures. 'No one is good—except God alone' (Mark 10:18).

Divine goodness is self-caused; it has no spring, for God possesses the whole nature of goodness in himself. There are no degrees to his goodness. Nothing can be added to it to make it better and nothing can be taken from it to make it wanting or defective. God is so good that he cannot be bad. He is immutably, eternally and infinitely good, holding in himself an inexhaustible and limitless treasure of goodness, enough to fill all things at all times anywhere in space. 'He is good; his love endures for ever' (2 Chronicles 5:13). 'Taste and see that the LORD is good' (Psalm 34:8).

a. The goodness of God in creation. The first manifestation of God's goodness outside of himself was at creation. 'God saw all that he had made, and it was very good' (Genesis 1:31). When he was alone in eternity, he contented himself with himself, abounding in his own blessedness and delighting in his abundance. At the beginning of time he revealed his goodness by creating. As creator, he is the author of all good and the only source of everything good in his creatures.

The Psalmist cries, 'I praise you because I am fearfully and wonderfully made; your works are wonderful, I know that full well' (Psalm 139:14). Our bodies consist of a variety of members, each one in due proportion to the others and designed for our good, without confusion, beautiful to behold, excellent for use and powerful in strength. The eyes, set back in the skull for protection, with eyelids to clean them, view the wonders of creation, all in perfect focus. The ears, so outwardly simple and yet through them we hear the pleasures of sound. The tongue, one of the smallest members and yet what learning it communicates. The hands, made so wisely to perform countless tasks. The feet, stable and strong, and able to carry us to wherever we choose to go. God is good and whatever he does is good.

b. The goodness of God towards his creatures. God's affection for his creatures causes him to seek their welfare and to provide for their needs (James 1:17; Matthew 7:11). His bounty moves him to deal kindly with them (Isaiah 63:7). He delights in his works and is beneficent to them, loving and caring for everything he has made (Psalm 145:13).

He upholds those who fall and lifts up all who are bowed down. He gives his creatures food at the proper time and his open hand satisfies the desires of every living thing (Psalm 145:14–16; cf 104:21). He clothes the lilies of the field and feeds the birds of the air (Matthew 6:26–29). He causes his sun to rise on the evil and the good, and sends rain on the righteous and the unrighteous (Matthew 5:45). He is kind to the ungrateful and wicked (Luke 6:35), and generous to the undeserving. He is the source of joy in his creatures and the promoter of their happiness (1 Kings 8:66; 1 Timothy 6:17). He is the fountain of all good (Psalm 36:9). 'The LORD is good to all' (Psalm 145:9). 'Let them give thanks to the LORD for his unfailing love and his wonderful deeds for men, for he satisfies the thirsty and fills the hungry with good things' (Psalm 107:8–9; cf 36:6; Acts 14:17).

He made man in his own image so he could enjoy communion with his creator, and set him in a richly furnished world for his benefit and pleasure. He gave him a law, designed for happiness and obedience, and entered into a covenant with him, promising an eternal reward. It is right to say that God produces all the happiness in the universe for the manifestation of his own glory, for his creatures' highest moral excellence, and for their highest blessedness in himself.

6. The love of God

God is not just loving, he is love itself. He is the personification of perfect love, which involves a responsible and faithful commitment to the well-being of his rational creatures. Love is the self-communication of God. God shares himself with his creatures, takes pleasure in the objects of his love, wills the good of all, and gives without complaint, regret or price. His love is expressed principally in the redemption of sinners. It can be defined as a spontaneous determination of God's whole being in an attitude of benevolence and benefaction that is freely chosen and firmly fixed. 'The LORD, the LORD, the compassionate and gracious God, slow to anger, abounding in love and faithfulness, maintaining love to thousands, and forgiving wickedness, rebellion and sin' (Exodus 34:6–7).

a. God's love is eternal and immutable. God has never existed apart from perfect love. Even before he manifested his love to his creatures, 'God is love' (1 John 4:8,16). He is eternal love because his eternal nature is love. He has no beginning and no end and therefore his love never fails. In the same sense God's love is immutable. No matter what happens around him, because there is no shadow of turning in his being, there is no change, for better or for worse, in his love.

b. God's love is sovereign. It is free, spontaneous and uncaused by anything outside himself. He loves his creatures because they are his creatures and because he has chosen to love them. He does not love them because they attract his love, for 'nothing good' (Romans 7:18) lives in them. 'All have turned away, they have together become worthless; there is no-one who does good, not even one' (Romans 3:12). He loves because it is his nature to love. 'The LORD did not set his affection on you and choose you because you were more numerous than other peoples, for you were the fewest of all peoples; but it was because the LORD loved you' (Deuteronomy 7:7–8).

c. God's love is infinite and holy. It is absolutely unrestricted and without a single defect. As far as the finite heart and mind of man are concerned, it 'surpasses knowledge' (Ephesians

3:18–19). Unlike his creatures' affections, God's love is not regulated by impulse or passion, but by principle, being pure and unmixed in both motive and action.

d. God loves unbelievers. God is perfect and therefore his love cannot find complete satisfaction in any object that is less than perfect. This means that he loves imperfect rational creatures for his own sake; that is, he loves himself in them, delighting in man as the reflection of his own image (Genesis 1:26–27). Since all men are made in his likeness, he loves all (Matthew 5:44–45), but not in the same sense. He loves unbelievers because they are his creatures, although he detests their sin and will punish them for it unless they obey the gospel.

e. God loves believers. God's children are the special objects of his love. It is to them that he communicates himself in the fullest and richest sense, making them the beneficiaries of his redeeming love and imparting to them the gift of eternal life (Romans 6:23). They are 'loved by God' (Romans 1:7; cf. 1 John 3:1) from whom nothing in all creation will be able to separate them (Romans 8:31–39). Before the creation of the world he chose them to be his own and set his fatherly affection on them (Ephesians 1:4; cf Jeremiah 31:3; Hebrews 12:5–11). For them all the promises of God are '"Yes" in Christ' (2 Corinthians 1:20) and to them every spiritual blessing and privilege flows (Ephesians 1:3).

The love of God is an exercise of his goodness towards individual sinners whereby he gives his Son to be their Saviour. 'This is how God showed his love among us: He sent his one and only Son into the world that we might live through him. This is love: not that we loved God, but that he loved us and sent his Son as an atoning sacrifice for our sins' (1 John 4:9–10). There was no greater gift that God could give, no higher demonstration of his love for lost mankind. Even if God created a million worlds for us to enjoy, such an act would not transcend or supersede the gift of his Son. 'While we were still sinners, Christ died for us' (Romans 5:8; cf Galatians 2:20; Ephesians 5:25) is glorious, matchless, divine love!

7. The grace of God

Grace is a favourable disposition towards the unworthy and wretched, and the free bestowal of kindness on one who has no claim to it. It is the exercise of love towards an inferior or dependent object and is commonly described as undeserved favour. God's grace is his unmerited goodness freely given to those who have forfeited it and who are, by nature, under the sentence of eternal death.

The grace of God is a self-existent principle inherent in the divine nature that appears to us as a self-caused tendency to pity the wretched, spare the guilty, welcome the outcast, and bring into favour those who before were under just disapproval. Divine grace means that God takes the initiative and seeks to communicate his favours and blessings to his creatures. He stoops to embrace the worthless and unattractive, and to bestow benefits on the undeserving.

a. The grace of God is eternal. Just as God's essence is eternal and immutable, so his unmerited love to man is from everlasting to everlasting and without the slightest hint of change. He has always been and will always be the 'God of all grace' (1 Peter 5:10). This grace was 'given us in Christ Jesus before the beginning of time' (2 Timothy 1:9) and will last through endless ages. It was planned before it was exercised, purposed before it was imparted, eternal before it was manifested.

b. The grace of God is free. Divine grace cannot be bought or won or claimed by right. It cannot be earned by the performance of religious and spiritual works, or secured by some excellence in man. It is not a matter of debt, for God no more owes a debt to fallen man than to fallen angels. If grace could be deserved, it would 'no longer be grace' (Romans 11:6). The truth is that God was under no obligation to pity our misery and repair our ruins; he could have justly left us to our fate.

Grace is divine love freely shown to guilty sinners, who deserve only eternal damnation. 'All have sinned and fall short of the glory of God, and are justified freely by his grace through the redemption that came by Christ Jesus' (Romans 3:23–24). Grace is both priceless and free—priceless in that it is beyond price, and free because nothing needs to be given in return for it.

c. The grace of God is sovereign. The unmerited favour of God rests on his sovereign will. It is dispensed according to his 'good pleasure' (Matthew 11:26; cf Romans 9:15) and bestowed on whoever he pleases (Exodus 33:19). No one is consulted by God as to the choice of the objects of grace and he is uninfluenced by the actions of his creatures. His grace cannot be resisted or extinguished, and it always accomplishes the purpose for which it was given. It is best demonstrated in the electing love of God that secured, at immeasurable cost, the blessedness of undeserving creatures.

d. The grace of God is fully revealed in Christ Jesus. It is perfectly manifested and exemplified in and by and through 'our Saviour, Christ Jesus' (2 Timothy 1:9–10). 'The law was given through Moses: grace and truth came through Jesus Christ' (John 1:17,14). As the 'radiance of God's glory and the exact representation of his being' (Hebrews 1:3), the Son of God is the perfect and complete expression of divine grace, and the channel through whom all the unmerited blessings of salvation flow. 'For if the many died by the trespass of the one man, how much more did God's grace and the gift that came by the grace of the one man, Jesus Christ, overflow to many!' (Romans 5:15; cf 5:17,21).

   e. The grace of God is bestowed on sinners for their eternal salvation. 'We believe it is through the grace of our Lord Jesus that we are saved' (Acts 15:11; cf Ephesians 2:5–9). The whole of salvation, from predestination to glorification, is for the 'praise of his glorious grace' (Ephesians 1:6; cf 1:12,14; 2:6–7). We are chosen by grace (Romans 11:6) and predestined to be adopted as his sons 'to the praise of his glorious grace, which he has freely given us in the One he loves' (Ephesians 1:5–6). We are pardoned 'in accordance with the riches of God's grace' (Ephesians 1:7) and 'justified freely by his grace' (Romans 3:24; cf 4:16; Titus 3:7).

   We are raised up with Christ in order that in the coming ages God 'might show the incomparable riches of his grace expressed in his kindness to us in Christ Jesus. For it is by grace you have been saved, through faith—and this not from yourselves, it is the gift of God—not by works, so that no one can boast' (Ephesians 2:8–9). Oh, amazing grace, so rich and free, and so able to save completely and eternally the worst of sinners (1 Timothy 1:14–15)!

8. The mercy of God

If grace is the love of God exercised towards the undeserving, then mercy is the kindness of God exercised towards the miserable. Grace freely gives unmerited benefits, while mercy modifies or withholds merited punishment. Because God is merciful 'he does not treat us as our sins deserve or repay us according to our iniquities' (Psalm 103:10).

   The two aspects of God's goodness can be distinguished by

saying that the grace of God contemplates man as guilty before God and therefore in need of forgiveness; and the mercy of God contemplates him as one who is bearing the consequences of sin, who is in a pitiful condition and who therefore needs divine help. The two attributes are often mentioned together (Nehemiah 9:31; 1 Timothy 1:2; 2 Timothy 1:2).

Mercy is the goodness of God, joined with a sentiment of pity, that is extended to the distressed or suffering, irrespective of their deserts. It presupposes sin and moves to relieve the misery that sin causes. In other words, divine mercy confronts human suffering and guilt, and disposes God to be actively compassionate, so that he pities the miserable and rescues them from trouble. 'In all their distress he too was distressed, and the angel of his presence saved them. In his love and mercy he redeemed them; he lifted them up and carried them all the days of old' (Isaiah 63:9). Mercy is sometimes called loving-kindness or tender compassion, because God is 'the Father of compassion and the God of all comfort, who comforts us in all our troubles' (2 Corinthians 1:3–4).

God's mercy is not incompatible with his justice because both perfections are equally and spontaneously in his nature. He is eternally and perfectly just and merciful. He therefore always dispenses his mercy justly. Nor is his mercy controlled in any way by the acts of his creatures, for nothing outside God obliges him to act. He is self-determining, regulating his mercy according to his own sovereign will. '"I will have mercy on whom I have mercy, and I will have compassion on whom I have compassion." It does not, therefore, depend on man's desire or effort, but on God's mercy' (Romans 9:15–16,18).

a. God's mercy is abundant. 'The Lord is full of compassion and mercy' (James 5:11). Divine mercy flows from a spring that no creature can measure or contain or comprehend. It is endless, exhaustless, 'very great' (1 Chronicles 21:13), stretching to the highest heavens and beyond, and, as far as his creatures are concerned, 'new every morning' (Lamentations 3:22–23). Such mercy is the reason for our salvation. God, who is 'rich in mercy, made us alive in Christ even when we were dead in transgressions' (Ephesians 2:4–5). 'He saved us, not because of the righteous things we had done, but because of his mercy' (Titus 3:5; cf 1 Peter 1:3–4). Now we are rightly called 'the objects of his mercy' (Romans 9:23).

b. God's mercy is eternal. It is a perfection of his eternal being and therefore ever flowing and never failing. It is a boundless, overwhelming immensity of divine pity and compassion that stands for ever. 'Give thanks to the LORD, for he is good; his love endures for ever' (1 Chronicles 16:34; cf 2 Chronicles 7:3; Psalm 136). 'His mercy extends to those who fear him, from generation to generation' (Luke 1:50; cf Psalm 103:17).

c. God's mercy is over all his works. 'The LORD is good to all; he has compassion on all he has made' (Psalm 145:9). God's mercy extends to his entire creation (Acts 17:25), so that all he has made receives appropriate and excellent blessings (Job 25:3; Matthew 5:45; Acts 14:17). 'He is kind to the ungrateful and wicked' (Luke 6:35–36) and takes no pleasure in their death, but entreats them to turn from their evil ways and live (Ezekiel 18:23,32; 33:11).

Although his mercy reaches into the life of every creature, it is especially shown 'to those who fear him' (Luke 1:50; cf Deuteronomy 7:9; Psalm 86:5). 'As a father has compassion on his children, so the LORD has compassion on those who fear him' (Psalm 103:13). On them his saving and everlasting mercy rests. It is right to say that believers have never yet been able to think of any real blessing that has not been secured to them by the God of mercy.

9. The patience of God

The patience or long-suffering of God is a further aspect of divine goodness. It is often thought of as the display or result of mercy, although the two perfections are essentially different. Mercy contemplates the creature as miserable because of sin, patience contemplates the creature as a sinner; mercy pities the miserable creature, patience bears with the sin that causes the misery; mercy makes God ready to receive returning sinners, patience makes him willing to bear with them in their sins. The two attributes are often mentioned alongside grace. 'But you, O LORD, are a compassionate and gracious God, slow to anger, abounding in love and faithfulness' (Psalm 86:15; cf 145:8; Exodus 34:6–7; Numbers 14:18).

The patience of God is that power of control which God exercises over himself, causing him to bear with the wicked and forbear so long in punishing them. God has complete control over himself. He is not at the command of passions, as men are, but can restrain his anger under just provocations to exercise it. 'The LORD is slow to anger' (Nahum 1:3; cf Nehemiah 9:17; Psalm 103:8). He is slow to anger, not for want of power to avenge himself because he is 'great in power' (Nahum 1:3), but because he possesses the power of self-restraint and self-control. His power is as great to punish as his patience is to spare, but he moderates and rules that power according to the holiness of his will. This enables him to suffer great injuries without avenging himself.

a. God is patient with impenitent sinners. When God's goodness is manifested to the guilty it is called forbearance or long-suffering. God is long-suffering in that he suffers evildoers for a long time without striking out against them. He is tolerant with the wicked, who repeatedly despise his admonitions and warnings, patiently bearing a multitude of provocations and graciously providing the offenders with undeserved temporal and spiritual benefits (Acts 14:16–17). He endures 'with great patience the objects of his wrath' (Romans 9:22).

This does not mean that God condones or ignores their sin, or that the wicked will escape punishment. God is simply postponing or withholding their merited, and often threatened, judgment (Romans 3:25), 'not wanting anyone to perish, but everyone to come to repentance' (2 Peter 3:9). Such patience shows the wicked that God is not an implacable enemy. He is appeaseable, if men seek his favour. 'Bear in mind that the Lord's patience means salvation' (2 Peter 3:15). 'Do you show contempt for the riches of his kindness, tolerance and patience, not realising that God's kindness leads you towards repentance?' (Romans 2:4).

b. God is patient with his own rebellious people. He does not cast them off when they err or crush them when they sin. He does not forsake them during periods of backsliding, but rather makes allowances for their frailties and pardons their evil conduct. He holds back his hand, not looking so much to what they deserve, as desiring to give place to his mercy, and being unwilling to use his strength against men who are so constituted as to live only for a short period in this world. 'He was merciful; he forgave their iniquities and did not destroy them. Time after time he restrained his anger and did not stir up his full wrath. He remembered that they were but flesh, a passing breeze that does not return' (Psalm 78:38–39; Ezekiel 20:17; Habakkuk 1:2–3; Matthew 23:37).

10. The holiness of God

The holiness of God is a general term that describes two aspects of God's being. The first points to God's absolute perfection in total glory. God is majestic in purity and altogether unapproachable, 'whom no one has seen or can see' (1 Timothy 6:16). He is the high and lofty One, who lives in a high and holy place, and whose name is holy (Isaiah 57:15; cf Hosea 11:9). He is far above all that is finite and imperfect, and absolutely distinct from every creature. 'Who among the gods is like you, O LORD? Who is like you—majestic in holiness, awesome in glory, working wonders?' (Exodus 15:11). This aspect of divine holiness represents his transcendence and venerable majesty, or the blessedness and nobleness of his nature.

When God's creatures comprehend the splendour of his holiness they bow low in worship, prostrating themselves in self-humiliation before the awe-inspiring majesty of his presence. They call with the seraphs: 'Holy, holy, holy is the LORD Almighty; the whole earth is full of his glory' (Isaiah 6:3; cf. Revelation 4:8). And they cry out with the prophet: 'Woe to me! I am ruined! For I am a man of unclean lips, and I live among a people of unclean lips, and my eyes have seen the King, the LORD Almighty' (Isaiah 6:5).

The Bible's emphasis on this aspect of God's holiness has led some to speak of it as God's central and supreme attribute. They call it his perfection of perfections and the glory of all the rest. In a strict sense all the perfections of God are equally essential and of primary importance. However, in support of the above, it is true to say that the holiness of God covers every facet of God's transcendental greatness and points to his 'Godness' more than all the other attributes. It is his greatest title of honour and a fuller expression of himself than anything else. His holiness is his glory, rendering him glorious in himself and glorious to his creatures.

The second aspect of divine holiness is God's infinite moral excellence. This can be discussed from a negative as well as from a positive point of view. Negatively, it conveys the idea of separation. God is eternally and in all ways perfectly free and separate from moral impurity. There is no moral blemish or defilement in his person and no mixture in his dealings with his creatures. 'God is light; in him there is no darkness at all' (1 John 1:5).

God cannot have communion with or take pleasure in sin (Psalm 5:4–6). He cannot encourage, command or perform evil in any way at any time. If he could, he would be acting contrary to his morally perfect nature. 'Far be it from God to do evil, from the Almighty to do wrong' (Job 34:10). He 'cannot be tempted by evil, nor does he tempt anyone' (James 1:13). He hates sin, whether inward or outward, with a perfect and intense hatred (Proverbs 6:16–19; 8:13; 15:9). 'Your eyes are too pure to look on evil; you cannot tolerate wrong' (Habakkuk 1:13).

Positively, it stresses the rectitude and integrity of the divine nature. God is absolute moral perfection, infinitely pure in every detail and without spot or blemish in any of his attributes, affections or actions. He is a lover of righteousness, goodness and truth, 'a holy God' (Joshua 24:19), who delights in his own purity and everything else that conforms to his law. He is 'the Holy One of Israel' (Isaiah 5:19; 30:12; 43:3; 55:5; cf Psalm 22:3), who demands holiness from his moral creatures. 'I am the LORD your God; consecrate yourselves and be holy, because I am holy' (Leviticus 11:44; 19:2; 1 Peter 1:15–16). 'It is God's will that you should be sanctified' (1 Thessalonians 4:3).

a. God's nature is holy. 'Holy, holy, holy is the Lord God

Almighty, who was and is, and is to come' (Revelation 4:8). God is essentially and necessarily holy, because holiness is the essential glory of his nature and as necessary to him as his being. Holiness is his essence.

God is morally spotless in character, untainted with evil desires, motives, thoughts, words or deeds. He is the absolute perfection of moral excellence, infinitely perfect in righteousness, purity, rectitude, and incomprehensible holiness. He is all over holy and the sum of all moral excellency is found in him. As his being is holiness, so are all his attributes holy, and he is the source, cause and standard of all that is right. 'I am the LORD, your Holy One' (Isaiah 43:15).

b. God alone is holy. 'There is no-one holy like the LORD; there is no-one besides you' (1 Samuel 2:2). There is no angel in heaven or creature on earth that is holy like God. Only God is infinitely, immutably and independently holy, and free from all limitation in his moral perfection. Such holiness is peculiar to him and incapable of expression in his creatures. He is holy from himself, holy in the highest degree, containing all the holiness of his creatures and infinitely more besides. Therefore, he is exalted in infinite majesty above all he has made, and absolutely distinct from all that is sinful and impure in the world. 'Who will not fear you, O Lord, and bring glory to your name? For you alone are holy' (Revelation 15:4).

c. God's words and works are holy. God is morally perfect in every operation he performs and in all his dealings with his creatures. As he can only act and speak according to his holy will, only the excellent proceeds from him. 'The LORD is righteous in all his ways' (Psalm 145:17; cf 18:30; 33:4). 'All nations will come and worship before you, for your righteous acts have been revealed' (Revelation 15:4). 'He is the Rock, his works are perfect, and all his ways are just. A faithful God who does no wrong, upright and just is he' (Deuteronomy 32:4).

The holiness of God is manifested in creation, when God saw that all he had made was 'very good' (Genesis 1:31); in the moral law that is written on man's heart and conscience (Romans 2:14–15); in God's holy law that forbids sin of any kind and demands from his creatures total adherence to its commandments; in the person and work of Christ Jesus, 'the Holy and Righteous One' (Acts 3:14; cf Mark 9:2–3; Luke 1:35), who is the highest and most perfect revelation of God's holiness; in the 'glorious gospel of the blessed God' (1 Timothy 1:11); in the church as the body of Christ; and in the daily judgments of God.

d. God's holiness is eternal and immutable. God has never attained perfect holiness or acquired it from another source, for he is eternally and unchangeably holy in himself, conforming only to his own standard of holiness. There are no degrees or shadows or blemishes in his perfect and infinite nature, and no possibility of his holiness diminishing or increasing. He is an incomprehensible fullness of eternal purity, whose essence is incapable of the slightest change. As he is immutably God from eternity, so he is immutably holy from eternity.

e. The holy God is the only object of reverence and worship. 'The LORD Almighty is the one you are to regard as holy, he is the one you are to fear, he is the one you are to dread' (Isaiah 8:13; cf Psalm 89:7). The Holy One of Israel, whose name is holy and awesome (Psalm 111:9), is alone worthy of adoration and honour. He is a 'consuming fire' (Hebrews 12:28–29), before whom men cower, gripped by a sense of their own self-emptiness and powerlessness. To see him makes even the strongest fall at his feet as though dead (Revelation 1:17). To be touched by him provokes cries of anguish from sinner and saint alike: 'Who can stand in the presence of the LORD, this holy God?' (1 Samuel 6:20). Come and worship his great and awesome name (Psalm 99:3). Exalt him in the sanctuary, bow low before his majesty, 'stand in awe of the God of Israel' (Isaiah 29:23). Give him 'praise and glory and wisdom and thanks and honour and power and strength … for ever and ever. Amen!' (Revelation 7:12).

11. The righteousness of God
Righteousness and holiness are closely related, the former being an expression or mode of the latter. Righteousness is a perfection considered in God's actions towards or upon his creatures, whereas holiness is a perfection considered absolutely in God's nature. Righteousness is strict adherence to law or conformity to a standard. God's person is his own absolute standard, which he never violates, and which he never allows his creatures to violate without requiring of them a full payment and satisfaction for sin. Holiness is the cause of righteousness and will not allow God to be unjust in himself or in his actions (Psalm 92:15; Hebrews 6:10).

God is essential righteousness, that is, his eternal essence is eternal righteousness (Psalm 111:3; 119:142; Isaiah 51:8). In other words, God is infinitely righteous in himself and in all his dealings with his creatures. He cannot enact an unjust law (Psalm 19:9; 119:137–138) or perform any action that is not perfectly holy and good. 'The LORD our God is righteous in everything he does' (Daniel 9:14; cf Psalm 145:17; Jeremiah 9:24). If he could act unrighteously, he would be acting contrary to his nature, which is absurd.

If a distinction is to be made between God's righteousness and his justice, then justice speaks of God as an impartial judge

(Psalm 96:13), who treats his creatures according to their deserts. It embodies the idea of moral equity, and is revealed in God's moral law and in the operation of his holy will. His judgment, which is the application of that equity to moral situations, is not arbitrary or inconsistent, but principled, fair and without respect of persons (2 Chronicles 19:7; 1 Peter 1:17; 2:23; Revelation 15:3; 16:5). God cannot condemn the innocent or acquit the guilty, nor does he punish with undue severity or forgive sins unjustly (1 John 1:9).

Another distinction can be made between the absolute and the relative justice of God. The absolute justice of God is the infinite moral perfection and universal righteousness of God's nature considered in itself. The relative justice of God is that perfection of God whereby he maintains himself over against every violation of his holiness, and reveals himself as the Holy One to his creatures. As the Holy One, God's infinitely righteous nature is exercised as the moral governor of his creatures, in the imposition of righteous laws and in their righteous execution.

In the Bible righteousness and justice are repeatedly ascribed to God. 'O LORD, God of Israel, you are righteous!' (Ezra 9:15; cf Nehemiah 9:8; Psalm 7:9; Isaiah 45:21; Jeremiah 12:1; Lamentations 1:18; John 17:25; 1 John 2:1,29; 3:7). 'The Lord, the righteous Judge' (2 Timothy 4:8). 'Righteousness and justice are the foundation of your throne' (Psalm 89:14). 'He is the Rock, his works are perfect, and all his ways are just. A faithful God who does no wrong, upright and just is he' (Deuteronomy 32:4; cf 2 Chronicles 12:6; Isaiah 30:18). 'Morning by morning he dispenses his justice' (Zephaniah 3:5).

a. The rectoral justice of God. The rectoral justice of God is the rectitude that God manifests as the righteous ruler and just judge of the world (Psalm 67:4; 99:4). He upholds the moral order in the world, executes his laws impartially, and governs his creatures and their actions with absolute fairness. 'The LORD is our judge; the LORD is our lawgiver; the LORD is our king, it is he who will save us' (Isaiah 33:22; cf James 4:12). As ruler and judge he has instituted a moral government in the world and imposed righteous laws on man (Deuteronomy 4:8). These holy, good and just laws, which are adhered to by him in the administration of his universal government, contain promises of reward for the obedient and threats of punishment for the disobedient (Romans 1:32).

b. The remunerative justice of God. This aspect of God's justice is part of his distributive justice, which relates to the righteous distribution of rewards and punishments. God will give to each person according to what he has done (Romans 2:6; cf Psalm 62:12; Proverbs 24:12; 2 Corinthians 5:10). 'To those who by persistence in doing good seek glory, honour and immortality, he will give eternal life. But for those who are self-seeking and who reject the truth and follow evil, there will be wrath and anger' (Romans 2:7–8; cf Isaiah 1:19–20; 3:10–11).

Remunerative justice manifests itself in the distribution of rewards. These rewards are given by God, not because his creatures deserve them (Luke 17:10; 1 Corinthians 4:7), for no one deserves anything good from God, but because he has promised to reward obedience. 'If you pay attention to these laws and are careful to follow them, then the LORD your God will keep his covenant of love with you, as he swore to your forefathers. He will love you and bless you and increase your numbers. He will bless the fruit of your womb, the crops of your land—your grain, new wine and oil—the calves of your herds and the lambs of your flocks in the land that he swore to your forefathers to give you. You will be blessed more than any other people' (Deuteronomy 7:12–14; cf Psalm 58:11; Micah 7:20; Romans 2:7).

These rewards are an act of divine grace, arising from the covenant relationship that God has established with the elect, whom he will eternally reward in heaven, not on the basis of their own merit, but on the basis of Christ's righteousness.

c. The retributive justice of God. Retributive justice is also called punitive or vindicatory justice. It is part of God's distributive justice and, as an expression of divine wrath, is displayed in the punishment of evildoers. 'There will be trouble and distress for every human being who does evil' (Romans 2:9; cf 1:32; 12:19). 'God is just: He will pay back trouble to those who trouble you.' 'He will punish those who do not obey the gospel of our Lord Jesus. They will be punished with everlasting destruction' (2 Thessalonians 1:6,8–9).

God's nature is eternal and essential righteousness, which means he is immutably obliged and determined to inflict on every sin an adequate and proportionate punishment. As a righteous judge (Psalm 7:11), who 'loves justice' (Isaiah 61:8), he must punish the wicked, and 'repay wrath to his enemies and retribution to his foes' (Isaiah 59:18).

God does not exercise retributive justice in order to reform the offender or to deter others from committing the same crime, for God acts independently, and finds the motive and end of his actions in himself and not in his creatures. He punishes sin because of the principles of his own nature and because such punishment is intrinsically righteous, and he hates sin because sin is intrinsically hateful. It is true that the punishment he inflicts may discourage others from sin, and it certainly provides a powerful incentive to live according to God's law, but these effects are secondary. God's primary objective in exercising retributive justice is to uphold righteousness.

d. The death of Jesus Christ. Divine justice was most gloriously displayed in the punishment that God inflicted on his own Son, Jesus Christ, for the forgiveness of sins (Isaiah 53:10; 1 John 2:2). 'He was pierced for our transgressions, he was crushed for our iniquities; the punishment that brought us peace was upon him, and by his wounds we are healed' (Isaiah 53:5). Jesus Christ not only suffered the penalty of the law vicariously, but he also fulfilled and obeyed its precepts on our behalf. He thus satisfied divine justice, which enabled God to be just in justifying the ungodly (Romans 3:25–26). In other words, thanks to Christ, the sinner's justification is judicially justified. (It is worth noting that the justice that saves the elect is the same justice that punishes the wicked.)

This satisfaction to the justice of God for the forgiveness of sins was absolutely necessary, for God is just and the justifier of him who believes. If sin could have been pardoned in some other way, without expiation, then 'Christ died for nothing' (Galatians 2:21); or if the law could have imparted life, then righteousness would certainly have come by the law (Galatians 3:21), and God would not have sacrificed his own Son.

12. The wrath of God

'The LORD is a jealous and avenging God; the LORD takes vengeance and is filled with wrath. The LORD takes vengeance on his foes and maintains his wrath against his enemies' (Nahum 1:2; cf 1:3–6; Deuteronomy 32:41–43).

God's wrath is a judicial and righteous hostility to sin, which manifests itself in frightful and yet just judgments against the wicked. God is the Holy One, who rages against the objects of his displeasure and indignation (Ephesians 2:3; cf John 3:36; Romans 9:22), pouring 'wrath on them like a flood of water' (Hosea 5:10). Wrath is the holy revulsion of God's being against all that contradicts his holiness.

The wrath of God is an expression of divine justice that arises from the eternal self-consistency of God's nature. It is a personal quality of the divine Being and the moving cause of the just sentences he passes on evildoers. It is rightfully called judicial because God, as judge, administers what strict justice requires. In these judgments God is never self-indulgent, arbitrary, fitful or subject to unstable, human emotions. Nor is he malicious or unnecessarily retaliatory. He is simply manifesting a right and necessary reaction to moral evil and expressing his eternal abhorrence of unrighteousness.

God's wrath is active in history in a threefold manner: in the righteous punishment of evildoers (Psalm 7:11; 78:31; 1 Thessalonians 2:16); in the judicial hardening of individuals; and in the withdrawal of restraints, when God hands men over in the sinful desires of their hearts to ever-increasing wickedness (Romans 1:24). 'God gave them over to shameful lusts … [and] to a depraved mind, to do what ought not to be done' (Romans 1:26,28).

The final manifestation of God's wrath will come at the end of the age, when 'the heavens will disappear with a roar; the elements will be destroyed by fire, and the earth and everything in it will be laid bare' (2 Peter 3:10). At that time the wicked will be thrown into hell 'where their worm does not die, and the fire is not quenched' (Mark 9:48); and the devil, that ancient serpent who deceived the nations, will be cast into the lake of burning sulphur to be 'tormented day and night for ever and ever' (Revelation 20:10). On that great and terrible day of the Lord only the elect, who have kept themselves pure, will be saved from wrath (1 Thessalonians 1:10; Romans 5:9).

13. The sovereignty of God

God upholds and sustains all things by his power, and determines the end they are to serve. He owns all things in heaven and earth (Deuteronomy 10:14; 1 Chronicles 29:11–12; Psalm 95:4–5; Ezekiel 18:4) and all things are subservient to and dependent on him. He rules as king in an absolute sense (Isaiah 52:7), and is clothed with unlimited and unconditional authority over all his creatures. He alone is God (Isaiah 45:5–6,21), exalted over all and unrivalled in majesty (Exodus 18:11).

God's sovereignty is displayed in creation, providence and redemption, as well as in his comprehensive plan for world history. He has established the laws by which his creatures are to live, determined their natures and powers, and assigned to them their appropriate sphere of service, position and lot. 'He determined the times set for them and the exact places where they should live … For in him we live and move and have our being' (Acts 17:26,28; cf Nehemiah 9:6).

The various names of God in the Bible emphasise his sovereignty: 'God Most High, Creator of heaven and earth' (Genesis 14:18–20); Sovereign LORD (Genesis 15:2); God Almighty (Genesis 17:1; Exodus 6:3); the Lord God Almighty (Revelation 4:8; 19:6); and 'the LORD Most High, the great King over all the earth' (Psalm 47:2; cf 47:8). Similarly, the names of the Son: 'Mighty God' (Isaiah 9:6), 'our only Sovereign and Lord' (Jude 4; cf Romans 10:9) and 'KING OF KINGS AND LORD OF LORDS' (Revelation 19:16).

Furthermore, the Son possesses all authority in heaven and on earth (Matthew 28:18) and holds a position that is 'far above all rule and authority, power and dominion, and every title that can be given, not only in the present age but also in the one to come' (Ephesians 1:21). He has a name that is above every other name, 'that at the name of Jesus every knee should bow, in heaven and on earth and under the earth, and every tongue confess that Jesus Christ is Lord, to the glory of God the Father' (Philippians 2:9–11).

a. The sovereignty of God is universal. God is the supreme ruler of the kingdoms of this world (Psalm 22:28; 103:19; 1 Timothy 6:15), and the only Lord of heaven and earth (Acts 17:24; Deuteronomy 10:14; 1 Chronicles 29:11–12; Psalm 95:4–5; Ezekiel 18:4). As such he establishes and directs human governments (Proverbs 21:1; Daniel 4:17,25; 5:21; Romans 13:1), saves the elect (Romans 8:29–30; 9:15–23; Ephesians 1:4–5), and determines man's life and destiny (Romans 15:32). Nothing resides outside his jurisdiction (Proverbs 16:33; Matthew 10:29) or beyond his dominion. Even the sufferings of Christ and the persecutions of Christians are under his sovereign control (Luke 22:42; Acts 2:23; 4:27–28; Philippians 1:29; 1 Peter 3:17).

God, in his sovereign distribution of his favours, gives to some riches, honour and health; while others are poor, unknown or the victims of disease. To some the light of the gospel is sent, while others are left in darkness. Some are saved through faith, others perish in unbelief.

b. The sovereignty of God is absolute. His authority is unlimited and unrestrained by anything outside himself. He is not subject to his creatures or influenced in any way by them. He does all that he pleases (Psalm 115:3; 135:6; Isaiah 46:10–11; Jeremiah 27:6) and none can stay his hand or thwart his plans (Job 42:2; Daniel 4:34–35). He is omnipotent and so easily able to keep his promises and carry out his decrees. However, in all that he does, he never violates his own character or purpose. His actions are controlled by his own infinite perfections, thus making him a wise, righteous, loving, holy, and powerful ruler. His absolute dominion not only guarantees the stability of the world, but is the ground of peace and confidence for the believer.

c. The sovereignty of God is eternal and immutable. It cannot be ignored, rejected, changed, usurped or extinguished, for it is an eternal dominion that binds all creatures. 'The LORD will reign for ever and ever' (Exodus 15:18). 'Your kingdom is an everlasting kingdom, and your dominion endures through all generations' (Psalm 145:13).

14. The power of God

God owns the strength to bring to pass, without effort or delay, his eternal purpose in exactly the way he purposed it; the ability to fulfil his promises without compromise; and the authority to do whatever he wills whenever he wills it. He can do whatever is possible to infinite, perfect power, even that which he has not decreed. God can, by the mere exercise of his will, bring to pass whatever he has decided to accomplish, and, if he so desired, do even more than that. This power to exercise his will is called omnipotence and it is an attribute of divine sovereignty.

God is the only all-powerful being. He therefore cannot be subject to another's dominion. He is the 'only Ruler, the King of kings and Lord of lords' (1 Timothy 6:15), who possesses in himself an inexhaustible reserve of incomprehensible power (Ephesians 1:19). Nothing is impossible with him or too difficult for his power to effect (Genesis 18:14; Jeremiah 32:27; Matthew 3:9; 19:26; Mark 14:36; Luke 1:37). He can do anything as easily as anything else. He speaks and it is done (Psalm 33:9). He never tires, but works continually and irresistibly (Job 9:4,12; Isaiah 43:13; Romans 9:15–21), and at his command lies the whole power of the universe.

His power is unlimited in range, absolutely perfect in mode and action, and without beginning or end. He is independent of everything outside himself and the source of all the power that is distinct in his creatures. He needs no instruments to act, but the instruments he does use receive all their power from him. All the power he requires to do all he wills lies in undiminished fullness in his own intimate being.

Although God is almighty (Genesis 17:1) and able to do all he wills, he cannot contradict his own nature or oppose his own will. He cannot do anything that is unbecoming to his holiness or goodness, or act in a manner that is unworthy of himself. For instance, he cannot deny himself (2 Timothy 2:13), or violate his word, or deceive his creatures (Numbers 23:19; Hebrews 6:18), for he is a God of faithfulness and truth. He cannot love sin or be tempted by evil (James 1:13), punish the innocent or change his nature (Romans 1:20; James 1:17). He cannot cease to be God, or deprive himself of life, or will anything that is not perfectly wise, holy and righteous. He cannot do what he cannot will. He abides by his own laws and all that he does is limited only by the perfection of his nature.

a. God's power is manifested in creation. 'Ah, Sovereign LORD, you have made the heavens and the earth by your great power and outstretched arm. Nothing is too hard for you' (Jeremiah 32:17; cf Isaiah 44:24). The whole of heaven and earth exhibit the greatness of God's eternal power (Romans 1:20). Out of nothing and by his word alone—that is, by the simple act of his will—the world and everything in it was formed. There was no existent matter for God to use, no instruments to assist him, no pattern or model for him to follow, and yet at his command, all things instantaneously and irrevocably came into being (Psalm 33:9; 148:5; Genesis 1:3).

b. God's power is manifested in providence. God is the first cause of all things and the governor of every secondary cause. In him all things live and move and have their being (Acts 17:28). He sustains all things by his powerful word (Hebrews 1:3) and satisfies the desires of every living creature (Psalm 145:13–16; cf 36:6). He delivers the church from her enemies, controls the devil and his agents, determines man's steps, and restrains the natural corruptions of the flesh. The whole creation is supported by his hand and directed to its appointed end.

c. God's power is manifested in redemption. Christ Jesus is the power of God (1 Corinthians 1:24), who rescues his chosen ones from the dominion of darkness and brings them into the kingdom of his Son, 'in whom we have redemption, the forgiveness of sins' (Colossians 1:14). It has rightly been said that the power of God glitters in redemption, whereby the devil is defeated in his designs, stripped of his spoils, and yoked in his strength; and that Christ, by his death on the cross, silenced the law, conquered death, pardoned sin and shut hell—the work of almighty power!

15. The will of God

Another attribute of divine sovereignty is the will of God. This is best described as God's power of self-determination, or his decree about what comes to pass. It is comprehensive, as all things are derived from his will (Psalm 135:6; Jeremiah 18:6), and includes his purpose, counsels and commands.

God's will is identical with his being and attributes, and an expression of his nature. It is the only rule for deciding right and wrong, and all his creatures are bound to be conformed to it. It is absolute and unconditional in both the means employed and the end accomplished, and the ground and cause of all things (Revelation 4:11), including all the acts of his creatures (Genesis 45:5–7; 50:20; Acts 2:23; 4:28).

a. God's will is eternal. God's will is one eternal, all-comprehensive act, absolutely determining either to effect or to permit all things past, present or future, in all their relations, conditions and successions.

b. God's will is free. God is uninfluenced by external causes and therefore absolutely independent of his creatures and their actions. He acts if and when he chooses, according to the laws of his own being, without any compulsion or obligation to any of his creatures. All that he does is determined by his own wisdom, goodness and sense of right. In the beginning he was free to create or not to create, to decree or not to decree. Since then he has been free to preserve the universe or to destroy it. This freedom is not a sign of indifference on God's part, but a rational self-determination within the divine being.

c. God's will is necessary. He cannot deny himself or will anything that is contrary to his being. He cannot change the nature of right and wrong, act unwisely or unrighteously, or create something that is self-contradictory. What he wills is always in perfect harmony with his other attributes.

d. God's will is decretive. This is the will of God's decree. God decrees all that comes to pass, either causatively or through the agency of his rational creatures (Daniel 4:17,25,32,35; Romans 9:18–19). The Shorter Catechism explains God's decree as his eternal and indivisible purpose, according to the counsel of his own will, whereby, for his own glory, he has foreordained whatever comes to pass (answer to question VII). God's decretive will is sometimes called his secret will because his eternal purpose is hidden in his own being and therefore known to him alone (Deuteronomy 29:29; Romans 11:33–34). Without the prophecies and promises in the Bible, God's secret will would only be known from its effects.

e. God's will is preceptive. This is the will of God's precept, the rule of duty for his rational creatures that is revealed in the law and in the gospel (Exodus 20:3–17; Deuteronomy 30:14; Matthew 5:3–11). As the moral governor of the world, God commands his moral creatures to do what is right and wise, and to obey his word (Matthew 12:50; Romans 10:8; 12:2). This aspect of God's will is sometimes called his revealed will because it makes known to us what infinite wisdom and goodness demand (Colossians 1:9–10; 1 Thessalonians 4:3–7), and represents the way in which we can enjoy the blessings of God (Deuteronomy 29:29).

The decretive and preceptive will of God, although they may appear distinct to us, are fundamentally one in God, and always in perfect harmony for God cannot decree what he forbids.

Conclusion

Oh, the depth of the riches of the wisdom and knowledge of God! How unsearchable his judgements, and his paths beyond tracing out! Who has known the mind of the Lord? Or who has been his counsellor? Who has ever given to God, that God should repay him? For from him and through him and to him are all things. To him be the glory for ever! Amen (Romans 11:33–36).

As I mentioned in the preface, my aim in writing on the divine perfections has been to give a more complete understanding of God, so that our worship of the Almighty Creator and Saviour of the world is based on a living reality. When we understand the glory of God's character, not only do we bow before him in reverence and awe, but we feel confident to approach the throne of grace, so that we might receive mercy and find grace to help us in our time of need.

For instance, when we know that God is a God of absolute and perfect truth, we know that all his promises to us are 'Yes' in Christ, and so through him the 'Amen' is spoken by us to his glory. We need never doubt anything he has ever said, because he cannot lie, nor does he change like shifting shadows.

When we know God's perfect love for us, it strengthens our assurance that no matter what happens to us in this life, nothing can affect the security of our eternal salvation. God will not withdraw his love from us, but will hold us in his hand through darkness and storms, through persecution and death. 'Can a mother forget the baby at her breast and have no compassion on the child she has borne? Though she may forget, I will not forget you!' promises the LORD (Isaiah 49:15).

When we understand the righteousness of God, we know that one day all the wrongs we daily see will be put right and, with the inhabitants of heaven, we shall sing the song of Moses and the song of the Lamb: 'Great and marvellous are your deeds, Lord God Almighty. Just and true are your ways, King of the ages. Who will not fear you, O Lord, and bring glory to your name? For you alone are holy. All nations will come and worship before you, for your righteous acts have been revealed' (Revelation 15:3–4).

When we understand the character of God and what his Son, Jesus Christ, has accomplished on the cross, it moves us to draw near to God as a child draws near to his father, without fear and in perfect peace; and it enables us to echo from our hearts the words of Isaiah: 'He tends his flock like a shepherd: He gathers the lambs in his arms and carries them close to his heart; he gently leads those that have young' (Isaiah 40:11).

To him who is able to keep you from falling and to present you before his glorious presence without fault and with great joy—to the only God our Saviour be glory, majesty, power and authority, through Jesus Christ our Lord, before all ages, now and forevermore! Amen (Jude 24–25).

ABSOLUTE: God is the first cause of all existing things, the ultimate ground of all reality and the one self-existent, eternal Being. He is free from conditions, limitations and restraints, and sustains no necessary relation to any other being.

ANTHROPOMORPHISM: the attribution of human characteristics, activities and emotions to God. It is a way of describing God in human terms, and a view of God that conceives of him as possessing or exercising attributes that are commonly found in his creatures.

ATONEMENT: the expiation of guilt by means of a vicarious sacrifice. Atonement propitiates God.

BEING: that which has a real, substantive existence. God's being is his essence or substance of which his perfections are the essential qualities.

COEXISTENT: existing together.

COGNITION: the act of knowing.

COMMUNICABLE: those attributes that are reflected in the lives of God's rational and moral creatures.

CORPOREAL: that which consists of bodily and material parts.

DECREES: the eternal purpose of God, according to the counsel of his will whereby, for his own glory, he has sovereignly and unchangeably foreordained all that comes to pass.

DEITY: God.

ESSENCE: the sum total of attributes that belong to and make up the fundamental and essential nature of God. These attributes cannot be removed from the divine being without destroying his essence.

ETERNAL: endless duration. God's essence is without beginning or end.

EXPIATION: the removal of guilt by vicarious punishment. The sinner's guilt was expiated when Jesus Christ died on the cross.

FOREKNOWLEDGE: in one simple and eternal act of cognition God knows all things.

FOREORDINATION: the act of God whereby, from all eternity, he has sovereignly determined all that comes to pass.

FREE: God's actions are uncaused by anything outside of himself.

GLORIFICATION: the act of God whereby all believers receive the full and final redemption of their bodies.

IMMANENCE: the nearness, presence and indwelling of God in creation. God is continually active in the world, sustaining and providing for all his creatures.

IMMENSITY: the infinitude of God's being in relation to space and viewed as belonging to his nature from eternity. God transcends all spatial limitations and is everywhere present with his whole being.

IMMORTAL: eternal existence. God is immune from death.

IMMUTABLE: God is unchanging in his being and purpose.

IMPASSIBLE: God is not capable of being acted upon or affected in any way by anything in creation.

INCARNATION: the term comes from a Latin word meaning 'to become flesh'. The eternal pre-existent Son of God became human in the person of Jesus Christ. 'The Word became flesh and lived for a while among us' (John 1:14).

A glossary of theological terms

INCOMMUNICABLE: those attributes that are uniquely God's.

INCOMPREHENSIBLE: the infinite God cannot be fully understood by his finite creatures.

INCORPOREAL: without bodily parts or physical matter.

INDEPENDENT: God has no origin and therefore does not depend on anyone or anything outside of himself for existence.

INFALLIBLE: incapable of erring.

INFINITE: God is without limits, imperfections or conditions.

JUSTIFICATION: the act of God, whereby he forgives all our sins and accepts us as righteous in his sight on the basis of Christ's righteousness, which is imputed to us and received by faith alone.

MOBILITY: God acts and moves in his world and among his creatures for his own glory.

NATURE: the quality or character of God.

NECESSARY: God is a necessary being in the sense that he needs nothing outside himself for existence.

OMNIPOTENCE: complete and perfect power is originally and essentially in the nature of God, enabling him to do whatever he pleases.

OMNIPRESENCE: the infinity of God in relation to his creatures. God is equally present with all his creatures at all times and in all places.

OMNISCIENCE: God knows all things.

PANTHEISM: the belief that everything is God. According to this view God is impersonal and identical with the universe.

PENALTY: suffering that is judicially inflicted in order to satisfy justice.

POLYTHEISM: a belief in a multitude of distinct and separate gods.

PREDESTINATION: from eternity God has determined and foreordained all that comes to pass.

PROPITIATION: the turning aside of divine wrath by the offering of a sacrifice. Jesus Christ removed God's wrath when he died on the cross as the atoning sacrifice for our sins (Romans 3:25; Hebrews 2:17; 1 John 2:2; 4:10).

PROVIDENCE: God governs and preserves all his creatures and their actions for his own glory. All things are ruled, not by chance or fate, but by God.

REDEMPTION: deliverance from sin and its penalty by the payment of a ransom. In Christ 'we have redemption through his blood, the forgiveness of sins, in accordance with the riches of God's grace' (Ephesians 1:7).

REVELATION: the act of God whereby he manifests himself and his will to his rational creatures. It is the communication of divine truth. The clearest revelation of God is Jesus Christ.

SATISFACTION: all that Christ has done to satisfy the demands of the law and the justice of God in the place and on behalf of sinners.

SELF-DETERMINATION: God is the author and cause of his own acts.

SELF-EXISTENCE: God does not depend on the world or anything in it for his existence. He is the uncreated cause of all things.

A glossary of theological terms

SELF-ORIGINATED: God, whose life is in himself, is the source and sustainer of all things.

SELF-SUFFICIENT: God possesses perfect power within himself to do whatever he wills.

SIMPLICITY: the persons in the godhead are numerically one essence and constitute one God, who is free from division into parts.

SOVEREIGN: God is by right the absolute and immutable king and ruler of the universe.

SUBSTANCE: the infinite, eternal and immutable being of God.

TRANSCENDENCE: God's distinction from and elevation above the world. God is beyond all finite reality and, as the self-existent one, detached from all his creatures. His activity and power are apart from the world.

VICARIOUS: Jesus Christ suffered in the place of sinners, assuming their obligation to satisfy divine justice.